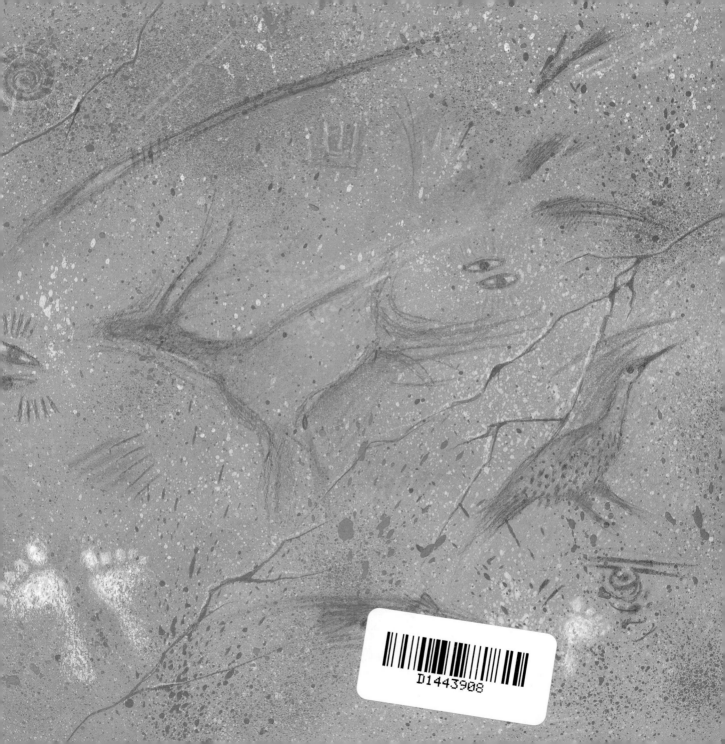

This book was created for
the International Year of the Family

*To Adriana and Francesca
and the Child's Play Family*

A proportion of the publisher's receipts will be donated
to the United Nations Fund
for the International Year of the Family
and selected family charities.

The First Family

by Michael Twinn

illustrated by Annie Kubler

Child's Play (International) Ltd

Swindon   Toronto   Sydney   New York

© M. Twinn 1994   ISBN 0–85953–936–9   Printed in Italy

Library of Congress number 94-21874

A catalogue reference for this book is available from the British Library

Was the woman big or small?
smooth or hairy? fair or dark?

Was the man strong or weak?
fast or slow? brave or timid?

Did they know each other or were they strangers?

Did they meet once or many times?

Were the man and the woman the first family?

Did they like each other?
Were they rough or gentle?
Did they know what they did?

Did the woman know she was carrying a child?

When the first child was born,
did the woman know where it came from?

Were the woman and the child the first family?

Was she alone or were others present?
Was she helped by other women?

Were they part of the first family?

The first child was helpless.
It cried for its mother.

It felt her.

Her face was the first thing that it saw.

Its mother felt its need and fed it ... and loved it.

Did the man know?
Was the man there?

Or did he come, when he heard the child cry?

When the man saw the child, how did he feel?

Was it then that he stayed?

Did the woman, the man and the child make the first family?

All families are not the same.
All children do not have a mother and a father.

But we all understand how the first family felt.

Ever since, in every land and in every nation, children are loved.

What makes a family?

Needing and caring, loving and giving make a family.

Talking and listening make a family.

Sharing and seeking make a family.

Let's be a family!